# EARTH MATERIALS AND SYSTEMS

# SOIL

by Keli Sipperley

T0084495

PEBBLE
a capstone imprint

Pebble Explore is published by Pebble, an imprint of Capstone.
1710 Roe Crest Drive
North Mankato, Minnesota 56003
www.capstonepub.com

**Library of Congress Cataloging-in-Publication Data**
Names: Sipperley, Keli, author.
Title: Soil / by Keli Sipperley.
Description: North Mankato, Minnesota : Capstone Press, [2021] | Series: Earth materials and systems | Includes bibliographical references and index. | Audience: Grades 4-6
Identifiers: LCCN 2020000836 (print) | LCCN 2020000837 (ebook) | ISBN 9781977123817 (hardcover) | ISBN 9781977126818 (paperback) | ISBN 9781977124180 (pdf)
Subjects: LCSH: Soils—Juvenile literature.
Classification: LCC S591.3 .S57 2021  (print) | LCC S591.3  (ebook) | DDC 631.4—dc23
LC record available at https://lccn.loc.gov/2020000836
LC ebook record available at https://lccn.loc.gov/2020000837

**Image Credits**
iStockphoto: Mumemories, 10, skynesher, 14, Tetiana Soares, 27; Shutterstock Images: Alex Lerner, 8, bluedog studio, 28, Elena Arkadova, 13, igorstevanovic, 5, Jennifer Larsen Morrow, 6, kram9, cover, La Renaissance Girl, 25, Ljubomir Trigubishyn, 22, Microgen, 18, Patila, 24, Richard Thornton, 11, Shyntartanya, 9, Slatan, 21, UniqueLight, 17
Design Elements: Shutterstock Images

**Editorial Credits**
Editor: Charly Haley; Designer: Jake Nordby; Production Specialist: Joshua Olson

All internet sites appearing in back matter were available and accurate when this book was sent to press.

# TABLE OF CONTENTS

Words in **bold** are in the glossary.

# What Is Soil?

Soil covers most of Earth's land. It is on the ground. We walk on it every day. Soil is sometimes called dirt.

All living things need soil. Soil feeds plants. Plants need the **nutrients** in soil to grow. Plants also need the water in soil.

Soil gives a home to many animals and bugs. It helps people make their homes too. We build houses and other buildings on soil.

Soil is made of air, water, **minerals**, and waste from plants and animals. Different kinds of soil have different minerals. There are many different kinds of soil.

One kind of soil is clay. Clay is heavier than other soils. It can hold a lot of water. It is lumpy and sticky when it is wet. It is hard like a rock when it is dry.

Another kind of soil is sand. Sand is lighter than other soils. It feels rougher than some other soils. It does not hold water or nutrients easily. Desert plants like cactuses grow in sand.

sand

loamy soil

Silt is another kind of soil. It is full of nutrients. It feels smooth. Many plants can grow in silt.

The best kind of soil for plants is loamy soil. It is a mix of clay, sand, and silt. Loamy soil has many nutrients.

## Where Is Soil?

Soil is all around us. It makes up the ground we walk on. Hills are made of soil and rocks.

Plants grow in soil. Soil holds the roots of big trees. There would be no forests without soil. People use soil to grow plants. We grow plants in gardens and on farms.

# How Does Earth Make Soil?

Soil is formed in **layers** underground. The layers are called horizons. Earth's soil was not all formed a long time ago. New soil is always being made. Each new layer of soil covers another.

It takes hundreds of years for Earth to make new soil. The minerals in soil come from rocks. Rocks are made of minerals. Heat and cold break rocks into tiny pieces over time. Wind and water break rocks too. These tiny pieces become part of soil.

layers

Another part of soil is waste from plants and animals. Leaves fall to the ground. Animals die. These things break down. They mix with the minerals from the rocks. They become part of soil.

Soil is not just rocks and dead things. There are living things in soil too. Most are too small to see with just our eyes. **Bacteria** live in soil.

There are some small living things in soil that we can see. Bugs live in soil.

The layers of soil form very slowly. In many soils the top layer is called humus. It is mostly made of rotting plants and dead animals.

Those dead things break down. They get buried. They become a second layer of soil. This layer is called topsoil. A new layer of humus forms above it. Topsoil is where plants grow best. The things that live in soil are in the topsoil.

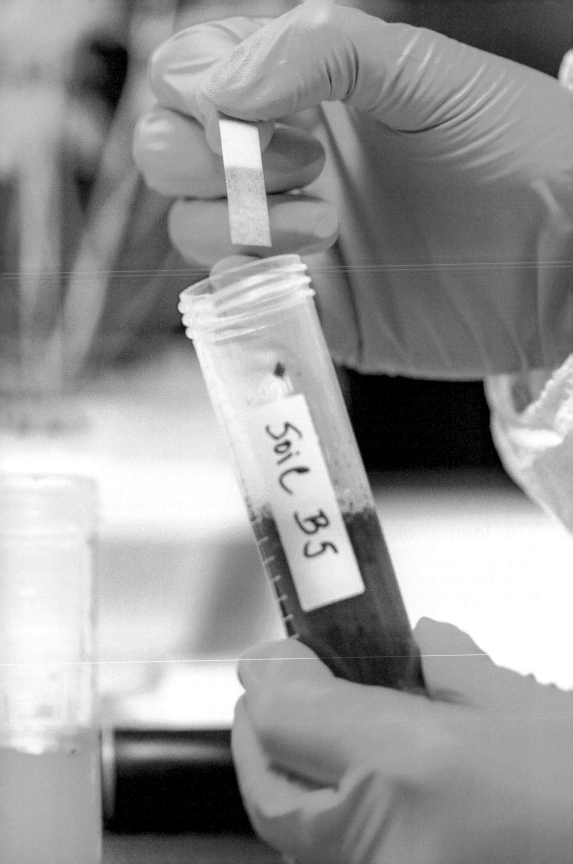

Below the topsoil is a layer called subsoil. This layer is made of clay. It has a lot of minerals.

At the bottom is a layer called bedrock. This is not soil. It is rock that sits deep within Earth under soil.

Scientists may study soil to learn about an area of land. They study the layers. They look at the dead plants in each layer. This can show what plants grew on that land.

# Why Is Soil Important?

Soil may seem like it just sits there. But it is actually hard at work. Soil does many important things.

Soil gives plants a place to grow. It holds their roots. It stores the water and nutrients that plants need.

We need plants. And we would not have them without soil. We eat plants as food. Plants also clean the air we breathe.

Soil gives homes to many living things. Millions of bacteria live in soil. **Fungi** live in soil too. Mold and mushrooms are types of fungi.

Bacteria and fungi break down waste in soil. This leaves nutrients that other living things can use. Plants need these nutrients.

Worms live in soil too. Moles and gophers are some of the bigger animals that call soil home.

worms

gopher

Other things live on top of soil. This includes us! Our homes are built on soil. Some things used to build houses come from soil too. Wood comes from trees that grow in soil. Soil is used to make cement and bricks.

Soil also helps take care of Earth's water. Rain and snow fall on soil. The soil soaks up the water like a sponge. The water could **flood** places if the soil did not soak it up.

Soil holds this water for living things to use. It helps clean our water too. Soil helps remove **pollutants** from water.

Soil is important for many living things. We could not live without it. Soil helps plants grow. Plants give us food and clean air. Soil cleans our water. It gives us a place to build our homes. So much of what we need starts with the soil under our feet.

# Glossary

**bacteria** (bac-TEER-ee-uh)—tiny living things that are all around

**flood** (FLUHD)—a disaster caused by water covering places it usually doesn't

**fungi** (FUHN-gye)—living things that are like plants but do not have leaves and are not green

**layer** (LAY-ur)—a thickness of something laid on top of another

**mineral** (MIN-ur-uhl)—a solid in the ground made by nature that is not a plant or animal; minerals are found in rocks and soil

**nutrient** (NOO-tree-uhnt)—something that plants and animals need to live and grow; people get nutrients from food

**pollutant** (puh-LOOT-uhnt)—something that makes water and air dirty and not safe to use

# Read More

James, Emily. *The Simple Science of Dirt*. North Mankato, MN: Capstone Press, 2018.

Orr, Tamra B. *Rocks*. North Mankato, MN: Capstone Press, 2021.

Sohn, Emily, and Diane Bair. *Pebbles, Sand, and Silt*. Chicago: Norwood House Press, 2020.

# Internet Sites

*Audubon: 10 Incredible Facts About Dirt*
https://www.audubon.org/news/10-incredible-facts-about-dirt

*DK Find Out!: Rocks and Minerals*
https://www.dkfindout.com/us/earth/rocks-and-minerals

*Soils4Kids*
https://www.soils4kids.org

# Index